DENE MICH

1st BUMPER BOOK OF CRAP JOKES

Publishers	5T Publishing Nemus House, 32 London Rd, Stockport, Cheshire SK7 4AH UK Email: info@5Tpublishing.com Tel: 0161 482 7800
Copyright	©Dene Michael
Design & Art Direction	Steve Collins
Artwork	Mark Goodwin
First published	2021
Reprint	10 9 8 7 6 5 4 3 2 1
ISBN	978-1-9161900-3-0

A catalogue record of this book
is available from the British Library

First Printed in Great Britain by 5T Publishing	2021
Designed and produced by 5T Publishing All rights reserved.	

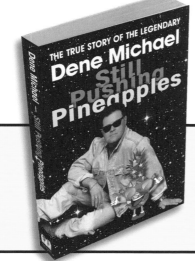

Hi everyone!

First of all I would like to thank you for buying my book of crap jokes.

People I meet seem to think I'm a bit of a comedian, well the thing is I can be quite funny when I'm fed a subject or two.
I have loads of jokes and many friends that are always asking me to tell them a joke. This is why I decided to write a book of jokes that bring back my memories of meeting and working with dozens of comedians during my time working in Benidorm, Spain.

Sadly, many of them have passed away now so this book is a tribute to my good comedian friends.

Lots of the same jokes are told by different comedians in the way that different singers sing the same song.
It's just the way the comic delivers the gag... and of course, that's the art of comedy.

I spent hundreds of hours sitting in dressing rooms back stage waiting for the comic to finish before I went on, and thats how I remember so many good and so many crap jokes. As the great Frank Carson used to say..
"its the way I tell 'em".

So, I hope you all enjoy this book... you can always hang it in the loo and whilst your sat there grab the book and have a laugh.

Happy chuckles everyone, kindest regards

Dene Michael.

P.S. if you have not already done so, please don't forget to read my life story... 'Still Pushing Pineapples'.

I was driving my Rolls Royce along the motorway when all of a sudden it wouldn't go above 30 miles an hour.
So, I pulled over and rang the breakdown service. I told them the problem and they asked me what gear I was in? I said, "..my wellies and donkey jacket!".

My girlfriend shouted downstairs to me from the bedroom - she was feeling a little fruity, and said..

'Shall I put some black lace on for you?'
I thought brilliant, I love a bit of AGADOO!

I bought some speaking scales the other day, I'm taking them back to the shop! I'm not being spoken to like that. I stood on them to weigh myself! They said one at a time please.

I had a black eye the other week. Someone said to me 'who's given you that black eye?' I said 'nobody has given me it, I've had to fight for it!'

I called into our local pet shop and I thought I would wind up the girl behind the counter. I said 'I've come to buy a wasp!' She looked at me funny and said 'we don't sell wasps!' I said 'well you had one in the window yesterday!'

So I opted for an African Grey Parrot. It was £50 or £75 with higher perches.

I was driving down the motorway and noticed a big lorry losing all his load, so I flashed my lights at him from behind. He wasn't taking any notice of me so I pulled up to the side of him and opened my window and shouted up to him.. 'You're losing your load, its all coming off the back of your vehicle!
He said, 'I'm a Gritter!'

I decided to go on holiday with a girl friend of mine a few weeks ago, we booked into what they described as a 5 star hotel! You could see 4 of the stars through the ceiling.. ha, ha, and I was the other one!.

The same hotel I'd just checked in with my girlfriend, she said "I don't like it here", I said "why?" She said "the room is so small, mirrors and signs everywhere and who are all these people in our room?"

I said "we're in the lift, sweetheart!"

I was sunbathing on the beach next to this beautiful girl, she said to me "would you like to see my white bits?" "Ohhh", I said, "would I!" So she took her rings off her fingers.

They said 'be careful it can be 100 degrees in the shade here'.. I said, "don't worry, it won't affect us! We are staying in the sun."

I was at the airport checking in at the desk.. the man said "put your cases on the scales!" He said "you're over weight!" I said "your ugly, but I can diet."

I was walking my pet in a gale the other day.. someone says to me "isn't it a bit windy for you to be flying a kite!"

I said "that's my dog!!!"

I was in Blackpool the other day and saw the Donkeys on the beach. I thought it was terrible what they gave them for dinner! Do you know what they gave them..? Half an hour!

One of the Elephants from Flamingoland zoo managed to escape and ran over the fields into the nearby village of Pickering, it ran down the Main Street and when it saw the jewellers shop it smashed its trunk through the window and sniffed all the rings and watches up its trunk and ran off! There were sirens and alarms going off..total panic! The police arrived and asked the little old lady who was passing at the time, what happened?

She told them what had happened and the policeman was writing it all down on his notepad. He said to the lady 'can you give me a description of the Elephant?' She laughed and said 'what do you mean, it was an elephant. He said 'yes, but was it an Indian elephant or an African elephant?' The lady said 'I don't know the difference!' The policeman said 'well an Indian elephant's ears stick up and an African elephant's ears droop down!'
'Oh', she said, 'I don't know..
this one had a stocking over its head.'

The same zoo had an apprentice learning how to feed the animals. After a few weeks, the curator of the zoo was going away on holiday and thought 'well the lad seems to be doing ok, I can leave him to it', and said to the boy, 'do you think you have it now, and can I rely on you to feed the animals whilst I'm away?' The lad said 'yes, no problem.'

He was on his own now and totally messed it up! He only fed the finch birds the wrong seed, and a few of them died! He thought 'the curator's going to go mad when he comes back!' He had an idea and thought.. 'if I feed them to the lions he will not miss them and I might get away with it.'

The next day he was feeding the chimpanzees and fed the wrong food to them, 2 of them died, he thought.. 'well I got away with it yesterday', so he fed them to the lions also. The next day he was driving the tractor in the bee field at the bottom of the park and only went and reversed into two of the bee hives and squashed all the bees. He thought 'OMG, I'll have to feed them to the lions too, no one will know.'

Anyway, the next day the zoo received a new lion to look after from another zoo, and the new lion said to the lions already there, 'Whats the food like in here?'

They said 'it blooming great! This week we've had *finch, chimps, and mushy bees.'*

Drunk man coming out of pub sees two Nuns walking towards him. They pass either side of him, he said to himself 'my God how the hell did she do that.'

Do you know theres so many empty beer bottles in the bottom of my garden it's put £200 on the value of my house.

I've sold one of my houses today, the council will go mad when they find out.

I've bought another house today its detached! Well its not really detached its just coming away from the other two in the terrace.

Little lad and his dad walking along the beach front at Blackpool they pass this lovely brand new rolls Royce car and little lad is scraping his spade up and down the side of the rolls Royce, dad says to the lad 'if you break that spade I'm not buying you another one'.

I wouldn't say my girlfriend is absent minded but she has to go to the shop everyday to buy a newspaper to see what day it is.

I said to my neighbour I was going to the newsagents to buy a paper and your dog went for me!

He said your very lucky he never goes for me.

Election of a new Pope in Italy.. they find the ideal candidate called Cardinal Sicola, but he had to be rejected because of his name. Imagine having a pope called Popesicola.

Farmer has a 'problem' with his sow. He's talking to his other farmer friend up at the farm next door. He said 'put it in your wheel barrow and wheel it up to my farm and we will put it with the boar and see what happens. If it's stood up and running about it's happened, if it's rolling in the grass, nothing's happened.

So, he does this every morning for a week, but nothing seems to be happening. It comes to the weekend and the farmer says to his wife 'look out of the window and see if the sow is laying on the grass or if its running about!'

She said 'its sat in the wheelbarrow.'

A woman is sat in the vets with her Alsatian dog, there's two other ladies there, also with their Alsatian dogs. They get talking whilst in the waiting room, she ask's the first lady 'what's wrong with your dog?' She says 'I'm having to have it put down, because its very vicious and biting people all the time'. She said, 'thats awful, I'm so sorry to hear that.'

She said to the 2nd lady 'what's wrong with your dog?' She answered, 'similar thing, every time the postman or milkman comes with a delivery, my dog bites them and they've complained, so I'm having to have it put down.' 'Thats awful', she said.

The ladies asked her why she had brought her dog in, and she replied 'well, every time I'm washing up at the sink it jumps up behind me and trys to hump me, and if I bend over to put the washing in the machine, it jumps on my back and tries to hump me!' The lady says, 'thats awful, having to have it put down for that!' She said, 'oh, I'm not having it put down, I'm having its nails clipped.'

14

I was staying in a hotel in Benidorm and was talking to the lady on the next balcony outside my room. We were on the 3rd floor and noticed she was cleaning her glass eye in her hanky. It slipped out of her hand and fell down towards the ground. A man was walking underneath and saw what had happened, he managed to grab hold of her false eye and took it up to her. She said 'thank you for that, it would have spoiled my holiday if it had broken and smashed.' She said to him 'let me buy you a drink!' He said 'I bet you say that to all the men don't you?' She said 'No! Only them that catch my eye.'

What is a little bear with no teeth called?

A gummy bear

I went to visit my doctors last week and my doctor said, 'my goodness, you've put some weight on during lockdown!' I said, 'I've had a lot on my plate lately.'

My mother is 87 and she was very ill the other day, I had to carry her to the kitchen to make my breakfast.

I was sat on the beach on a deck chair and a man came up to me and said 'hey, 10 euros for the deck chair!' I thought well thats not bad they are about £30 in Wilco.

My girlfriend and I were lucky enough to go on a cruise. One day she went missing and I said to the Irish captain, 'have you seen my girlfriend? He said to me, 'I think she's gone to listen to the band.' I said, 'how do you know that?' He said 'there was a message came over the tannoy 'abandon ship', and she went running off to see them.'

16

I was sat in a bar chatting to my friend and said to him I've given up smoking, women, and drinking.

Its been the longest 20 mins of my life so far.

I was making love to my girlfriend the other day, she's getting so lazy, I said to her 'did I hurt you then?' She said 'no!'
I said, 'I could have sworn you moved.'

Another time I went shopping for myself and put some food in my trolly.. 2 sausages, 2 eggs, 2 slices of bacon, 1 small tin of beans. The lady at the till said 'awww, you live on your own don't you?' I said 'yes, you can probably tell with what I'm buying!' She said 'no, your an ugly sod.'

I went shopping for Mum at Christmas and she phoned me and said 'can you get me a leg of lamb?'

I forgot to put it on the list. I said 'Mum the trolly is full, but I'll go back to the meat aisle and see if I can get one.'

I couldn't fit it into the trolly as it was full so I put it under my arm and proceeded to the check-out. It was so busy and I forgot about the leg of lamb under my arm and walked out of the door.

The security man came running after me and shouted 'hey you, what are you doing with that leg of lamb?'
I said 'boiled potatoes, cabbage, yorkshire pudding.. the whole shebang!

I took Mum on holiday last year, we went for two weeks. The first week we were half board, and the 2nd week we cheered up a bit.

I was hitch hiking the other day to Bradford, it was very foggy and I got into this car that had stopped for me, it was going very slowly and I noticed it had no driver. When it stopped I jumped out and this man got into it. I said to him 'there's something wrong with that car!' He said 'I know, I've just pushed it all the way from Leeds.'

I wouldn't say I was an ugly baby but when the ladies used to come and look into my pram they usually say, 'what a lovely baby!' But, in my case they said.. 'ohhh, what a lovely pram.'

The police stopped me in my car the other day and said to me 'your drunk!' I said 'I'm not drunk!'. He's said to me 'yes, you are drunk, I can smell the alcohol on you!'
He was being very clever with me and said to me 'been drinking, have we?
So I said 'well, I have, but I don't remember buying you one!'

The teacher asks little scouser Jonny 'where's Sara-wak? Little Jonny replied 'I don't know, cock.'

A police woman stopped me in my car and said 'get out of the car your drunk.' I said 'I can't be, I haven't been drinking', she said 'you were all over the road. Get out of the car, now walk down that white line at the side of the road'. I did and she said 'there you go you're staggering'. I said 'you're not so bad looking yourself'.

What do you call a Skoda with a sun roof?

A skip.

What do you call a Skoda with an Aerial?

A dodgem

Where do sheep go to get a haircut?

The baa baa shop

How do you double the price of a Skoda?

Fill it with petrol.

I recently went on a coach mystery tour and paid £5 to enter the quiz to see who could guess where we were going to.

The coach driver won it.

My Grandfather was a coach driver. I hope I die like my Grandad did, peacefully in his sleep.. not like his 52 passengers, all kicking and screaming.

My other grandfather was a tough guy, he used to be a bare knuckle fighter. He had engraved on his grave, 'who are you looking at?'

My girlfriend this morning was frying one of my socks in the frying pan when I woke up.
I said 'what are you doing?'
She said 'last night when you were drunk, you asked me to cook your sock!!!'

Knock knock,
who's there?
Amos,
Amos who?
A mosquito.

Knock knock,
who's there?
Anne.
Anne who?
Another
mosquito.

Knock knock,
who's there?
Helen,
Helen who?
Hell another
mosquito.

Knock knock.
Who's there?
Arga?
Arga who?
Agadoo do do.

Knock knock,
who's there?
Butcher,
Butcher who?
Butcher left arm
in, ya left arm out.
in, out, in, out,
shake it all about.

Knock knock,
who's there?
Wurlitzer,
Wurlitzer who?
Wurlitzer one
for the money
two for the
show...

Knock knock,
who's there?
Oh you've
heard it!

I called in the Butchers the other day and they had a sign in the window with a special offer.

It said two pork pies for £1. I wasn't very hungry so I went into the shop and said 'how much is it for 1 pork pie then?' They said it was 75 pence for one, I said 'I'll have the other one then'.

I bought 2 gold fish the other day for my son, he called one of them 1 and the other one 2.

I said 'why have you done that?' He said, 'if one dies I've still got two'.

I went to the doctors yesterday and said 'you are going to have to help me!' He said 'why?' I said 'I keep thinking I'm a supermarket!' He said 'how long have you been feeling like this?' I said 'ever since I was Lidl.'

I wrang the doctor the other day and said 'I keep feeling like I'm a pair of curtains', he said 'oh come on pull your self together'.

I wrang the doctors the other day and said to him I can't stop singing Tom Jones songs! Every morning when I wake up I'm singing the Green Green Grass of Home. Before I go to sleep I find my self singing My My My Delilah!
He said, 'well thats not unusual'.

26

I said 'doctor I keep thinking I'm a banana?' He said 'why is that?' I said 'I'm not peeling well.'

Why do bagpipers walk when they play?

To get away from the noise.

I wouldn't say my friend is tight but she turns the gas off to turn the bacon over.

When I'm on stage... sweeping it, I wear flip flops so when I walk off it sounds like a round of applause.

What do you call a woman with a storm on her head?

Gale

My girlfriend was cooking me a lovely meal last night, I could hear pots and pans banging, she was in there for 2 hours. I thought wow this in going to be a nice meal. When she brought it out to me it was spaghetti hoops.

5am this morning in the apartment we were staying at, the people upstairs were moving and banging furniture about, I couldn't hear myself drumming, it was so loud!

She said to the landlord of the pub do you have a big black dog with a white collar?
He said 'no'. She said 'have you got a big black cat with a white collar?' He said 'no'. She said to me 'there you go I told you it was the vicar I ran over'.

The other day I had laryngitis and went to the doctors I whispered to the nurse in the doctors surgery, "is the doctor in", she whispered back, "no, he's not!!! Come in!!!"

I went to the dentist the other day and said 'how much is it for 4 teeth taking out?' He said '£500', I said, 'wow, thats expensive, can you just slacken them for me, I'll take them out myself'.

When we play dominoes in the pub she dare not knock in case the waiter comes over.

What do you call a woman with a tortoise on her head?

Shelley

What's brown and hairy and wears sunglasses?

A coconut on holiday.

I rang another dentist and said 'how much is it for a tooth taking out?' He said we have 3 prices! I said 'whats the prices then?' He said 'well for £100 I can give gas and air'. I said 'is it painful?' He said 'no not at all'.

I said 'whats your next price?' He said '£50, I give an injection and do it that way'. I said 'is that painful?' He said 'it hurts a bit when I put the needle in and its a bit sore after.'

I said 'whats your other price?' He said 'for £5 I can take it out, no gas, no injection, just pull it out.' I said 'does that hurt?' He said 'yes, very much so, it's excruciating!'

I said 'I'll have the £5 one, book my girlfriend in for this Friday.'

The police stopped me one day and said I was speeding! They said I was doing 50 miles an hour in a 30 miles an hour limit. I said I can't have been! I've not even been out an hour!

My best mate went completely bald about ten years ago, but he still carries a comb with him. He just can't part with it.

I was horrified when my wife told me that our five year old daughter wasn't actually mine.

Apparently I need to pay more attention when I pick her up from school!

I took another girl home once to meet my parents. When she got up to go to the toilet my dad whispered to me 'omg, she's a bit rough isn't she? Not your usual type.' I said 'what do you mean?' He said 'well, she's rather big, warts, spots, no hair, no teeth and a false leg and arm!'

I said 'theres no need to whisper she's deaf.'

What is the best cure for water on the brain?

A tap on the head.

I went to a restaurant for a job as a chef recently, the head chef said 'how much experience do you have with eggs?' I said, 'just give me an egg and I'll show you.' I took the egg threw it up in the air onto my right shoulder, flipped it across to my left shoulder, flipped it in the air again onto my left foot across to my right foot flipped it back into the air, the egg came down hit the frying pan on the edge, the shell split in half and shell fell into a bin below, the egg into the pan and started cooking. He said 'thats amazing!!! Can you do that again?' I said 'yes' and repeated the process again.. he couldn't believe it. I said 'well do I get the job then?' He said 'no you mess about too much.'

I went to the doctors and said to him 'my brother keeps thinking he's an Orange.' He said 'well tell him to come and see me then', I said 'I've brought him with me! He's in my pocket.'

The man that wrote the hokey-cokey died last week, it took them 6 hours to get him into the coffin! Every time they put his left arm in the right one came out, then they put his right leg in and the left one came out.

I had a problem with the hokey-cokey, but it turned out that that's what it's all about!

What musical instrument can be used to catch a fish?

A castanet

A man is getting an assessment to leave the lunatic asylum, he's been there for 10 years. The man says to him 'what do you want to do when you leave here?' He said 'what do you mean?' He said 'well you've been learning to be a Plumber whilst you been in here, you could do that!' He said 'you've also been learning to be a Mechanic whilst in here, you could choose that. Or stay in here and be what you've always been.' Whats that? he says. A teapot.

What did the mayonnaise say when the refrigerator door was opened?

Err, do you mind, I'm dressing!

Little boy comes running in to his mum and says 'mummy, mummy, how do buffaloes make love?' She says 'I don't know, your fathers a Mason.'

Teenager comes in from school and says to his dad 'I'm sure my maths teacher fancies me.'
Dad says, 'why's that son?'
'Well, she keeps putting kisses next to my sums.'

Spelling teacher asks the kids to spell Thistledown. They all attempt it and one lad gets it correct. Teacher says 'now tell me what Thistledown means!' He says 'raining very heavily.'

Had a call from my local fish shop asking me to do a charity show, I said 'what's it to raise money for?'
They said, 'battered fish.'

Had a call from local fire brigade to do a charity show, when I arrived there to do it, it was a hoax.

I was doing a gig last week and the man that booked me said 'I hope you have got a good memory for faces!' I said 'why?'
He said 'there is no mirror in the dressing room.'

I went to the psychiatrist the other day and said 'I keep thinking I'm a dog'.
He said, 'just pop up on the couch and we'll talk about it.'
I said, 'I can't, I'm not allowed on the furniture!'

Doctor, Doctor, people are ignoring me all the time, and it's driving me crazy.

'NEXT..!'

'Doctor, Doctor, I keep thinking I'm a pair of curtains.'

'Stop being stupid, and pull yourself together'.

What did the fish say when it swam into a wall?

'DAM'

What do you call a can opener that doesn't work?

A CAN'T opener

Two muffins were sitting in the oven, one turned to the other and said,
'blimey, it's hot in here'.
The other one said,
'bloody hell, a talking muffin!

What's the difference between a rabbit and a banana?

They're both yellow, apart from the rabbit.. obviously!

What's red and bad for your teeth?

A brick.

A man walks into a bar with a giraffe. After a few drinks the giraffe keeled over and died. The man begins to walk out of the bar and the bar tender stops him and said 'you can't leave that lyin' there'.
The man turned around and said 'it's not a lion mate, it's a giraffe!'

I said to this fella walking his dog this morning, 'why is your dog wearing brown boots?'

He said, 'his black ones are being mended.'

Fred West being interviewed by the police - they ask him how many people does he think he's killed? Fred says 'I'm not sure, but I think it's seven.'
The police say 'but, we've already found twelve.' Fred says 'yeah, well I'm a builder and that was only an estimate'.

I lent my friend £5000 to have his face done in Harley Street. I don't know what he looks like now to get my money back.

My mate has a long miserable face, I say to him 'whats wrong?'
He says, 'I don't want to go home'. I say 'why?'
He says 'it smells horrible in our house and I can't bear it anymore.'
I say 'why's that?'
He says 'my wife has lots of cats and the smell, its getting worse.'

I said 'well, why don't you open the windows?'
He says 'what and let all my pigeons out !!!!'

Woman of 87 goes to the doctors and says 'there is something wrong with my left knee can you examine it please?' He checks it and says 'all I can put it down to is old age'. She says well my right knee is the same age and there's nothing wrong with that one.'

I was just doing my hair this morning and thought to myself 'I'll make it smell nice', so I thought I would put some toilet water on it.. the bloody seat fell down on my head.

Man takes his dog to the vets to be put down, I said to him 'is it mad?' He says, 'well its not very happy.'

Fella walks in to shoe shop to buy a pair of tortoise shell shoes - he bought them and put them on. It took him two hours to walk out of the shop.

I wouldn't say that I was ugly as a child, but if I'd have stayed at Michael Jacksons ranch I would have had a room on my own.

Fella in prison said to the warden, 'its cold in this cell'. A prison officer called out.. 'hang on, I'll put another bar on.'

A man gets a call from the telephone company saying he hasn't paid his bill. The man says 'oh, don't worry about that, I've placed it in a queue'.

I was talking to a guy with a foreign accent on the railway station platform, and he was holding a very long pole, so I asked him 'are you a pole vaulter?'. He said, nein, I am German, but how did you know my name is Walter?

Do you know when there's a knock at the door or the doorbell rings, why does the dog always think it's for him?

It doesn't matter how wet and cold you are as long as you're warm and dry!!!

I went to the army and navy store to buy a camouflage jacket. They said they had 500 of them, but couldn't find them.

I walked into a tailors and asked 'do you have a suit to fit me off the peg?' They said 'if we have, someone is for the sack!'

I'd never cheat with another woman because I really love my house.

New divorced barbie doll - £350 comes with Ken's house, Ken's car, and half of Ken's bank account.

I'm not going to get married again I'm just going to find a woman I can't stand and give her a £100,000!

Paddy and Murphy on holiday in Africa on safari. Paddy runs up to a lion sleeping on the grass and kicks it right hard in the goolies. Paddy says to Murphy, 'quick, run, its waking up! Murphy says, 'I'm not running, I didn't kick it.'

Guy walks into a psychiatrist with a rasher of bacon on his head, a sausage on each shoulder and a fried egg on each foot.. Psychiatrist says, 'and what can I do for you sir?'
The guy says 'I'm fine, I've come to see you about my brother!'

My grandad gave all his money away to sick horses!
He didn't know they were sick when he bet on them.

I asked my mum what the difference was between a Bison and a Buffalo, she said 'you can't wash your face in a buffalo'.

What do you call a small river that flows into the Nile?

A juvenile

Woman goes to hospital for a hip replacement and says to the surgeon, 'could I have the bone for the dog please?'

If I'd not been a singer/musician, I would have been a doctor, but I didn't have the patients.

Fella walks into the doctor and says to him 'I can't stop telling lies'. The doctor says to him 'I don't believe you.'

My girlfriend said to me 'take me out tonight somewhere expensive please, you haven't taken me out for a long time', I said 'ok dear'.. so I took her to the petrol station.

After that I also took her out for tea and biscuits... its the first time she's been a blood donor.

I bought a new stage shirt yesterday from a shop that sells seconds - it said this product may have a slight flaw on the label.
When I got it home one of the sleeves was 2 inches shorter than the other 2 sleeves.

My friend in Spain failed his driving test today, he forgot to double park on a zebra crossing .

I went to the cobblers the other day, and said to him 'I would like these boots soled.' I went back the next day and he gave me £20, he said 'I've sold them for you.'

I have started a shoe recycling business... it's absolutely sole destroying.

I bought a new helicopter business, but it never took off .

My friend asked me to bring him some cigarettes back from my holiday, I said how many would you like? He said 'bring me 10 cartons back please.' When I arrived back from my holiday he said 'did you bring my cigs back, and how much do I owe you?' I said, 'yes, and you owe me £1750'. 'OMG', he said, 'where have you been?' I said 'Scarborough'.

I had an origami business but that folded.

I went on a rollercoaster ride with my friend Brian, I said 'if we go upside down will we fall out?', he said 'no, we will still be mates'.

Two local criminals - one stole a lorry full of fireworks and the other one a pallet full of car batteries, the police charged one of them and the one that stole the fireworks they let off.

A truck load of viagra was stolen. Police are looking for hardened criminals.

You can now buy Viagra eye drops, it does nothing for your willy, but it makes you look hard.

Did you know that the famous actor Yul Brynner was a secret Liverpool fan and never wore aftershave? Yep.. Yul never wore Cologne.

There was a massive queue outside Waterstones last week, I thought, 'that's a turn up for the books'.

I phoned B&Q the other day and said to the guy 'how big's the queue mate?' and he said 'same size as the B, mate!'

I bought a book called superglue! I couldn't put it down.

I've just finished building a racing car entirely from spaghetti.
My girlfriend just laughed at me...
should have seen her face when I drove Pasta.

In which country are you most likely to slip and fall over?

Greece

Which vegetable goes best with jacket potatoes?

Button mushrooms

Why do seagulls fly over the see?
Because if they flew over the bay they'd be bagels.

Why do milking stools only have three legs? 'Cos the cows got the udder.

What did Batman say to Robin before they got into the Batmobile?
Get into the Batmobile Robin.

Wife with a big smile on her face says to husband 'I've managed to reverse the car out of the garage this morning', he replies 'thats not good, I reversed it in last night.'

A lady at the front row of my concert had lovely teeth, I commented over the microphone 'haven't you got lovely teeth?' She smiled at me, and I said 'take them out, hold them up and show everyone.'

My daughter thinks I don't give her enough privacy.

At least that's what it says in her diary!

Boomerangs are Australia's biggest export, but strangely, they are also it's biggest import.

Do you remember the joke I told you about my spine? It was about a week back.

I was in Manchester airport and there was an announcement over the tannoy.. 'the plane to Dublin will leave at 17.30 and for all the Irish people it will leave when the big hand is on 5 and the little hand is on 6.'

I walked into a tailor's shop and said 'I'd like to try that suit on in the window, 'he's said 'you can't, you will have to try it on in the cubicle fitting room like everyone else.'

Irish man was struck with lightning! He thought he was having his photo taken.

A priest was seated next to an Irishman on a flight from London to New York.

After the plane was airborne, drink orders were taken. The Irishman asked for a whiskey, which the attendant brought to him.

The flight attendant then asked the priest if he would like a drink. He replied in disgust, "I'd rather be savagely raped by a dozen whores than let liquor touch my lips."

The Irishman then handed his drink back to the attendant and said, "Me, too, I didn't know we had a choice."

Teacher at Sunday school class says 'can anyone tell me where Jesus lives? A little girl puts her hand up and says, 'in our bathroom!!!' Teacher says 'hows that?' Little girl says 'well every morning when my dad goes to use the bathroom and hammers on the door, he says, 'Jesus, you still in there??!!'

Man goes into doctors and says 'I keep thinking I'm a bell!' Doc says 'well go home and have a lie down, and if you don't feel better soon give me a ring.'

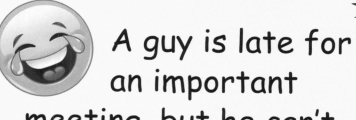

A guy is late for an important meeting, but he can't find a place to park.
In desperation, he begins to pray.
"Please Lord, if you help me find a parking bay right now, I promise to go to church every Sunday and never drink vodka again!"
A moment later, he sees a beautiful empty spot right next to the entrance.

"Never mind. Found one!"

A woman has twins and gives them up for adoption.

One of them goes to a family in Egypt and is named Amal. The other goes to a family in Spain. They name him Juan.

Years later, Juan sends a picture of himself to his birth mother. Upon receiving the picture, she tells her husband that she wishes she also had a picture of Amal.

He responds,
"They're twins! If you've seen Juan, you've seen Amal."

Two spanish firemen...
Hose A and Hose B

A guy goes to a psychiatrist. "Doc, I keep having these alternating, recurring dreams. First I'm a teepee, then I'm a wigwam, then I'm a teepee, then I'm a wigwam. It's driving me crazy. What's wrong with me?"

The doctor replies, "It's very simple. You're two tents."

Name the days of the week beginning with T.

Answer: Today and Tomorrow.

I used to manage the 5 Nolan sisters, now I can only manage one of them!

A man goes for a job as a litter collector, boss says 'have you any experience?' He says 'no I'll pick it up as I go along.'

My girlfriend talks through here nose. Her mouth's worn out.

I landed at Belfast airport and wanted to know the quickest way to the city from the airport so I asked the Irish taxi driver and he said 'are you walking or are you driving?' I said 'I'm driving!' He said 'well thats the quickest way.'

Did you know that Chinese women never have a headache? Thats why there's 1000,000,000 of them!

Man goes into the doctors and says 'can you give me something to make me sweat?' Doc says, 'yes' and signed him off the sick.

Whats the difference between a rottweiller peeing up your leg and a Yorkshire terrier peeing up your leg?

Answer - you let the rottweiller finish!

I said to my friend 'I have some bad news from my doctor! I have to take tablets for the rest of my life.' My friend said, 'well that's not so bad!' I said, he's only given me 4 tablets.'

I went to my doctors for a check up, he said to me 'how are you feeling now?' I said 'just like my new vacuum, picking up nicely.'

My friend is being cremated next week, but, unfortunately I can't get there at the time of the cremation, so I've asked them to keep him on a low gas until I can get there.

3 men get stranded on a desert island - an English, a Scotsman and an Irish man. A genie appears and grants them a wish each.
One man says 'I wish I was back in Scotland drinking whisky with my mates', quick as a flash he's gone his wish was granted.
2nd man from England says 'I wish I was at Wembley playing football with my team', quick as a flash he's gone.
Irish man looks round and says I wish my two friends were back here with me!!!

Two men stuck on a desert island after being shipwrecked.. I wouldn't say they were unlucky, but the Titanic sailed by and picked them up to save them .

How long can you keep a chicken in a freezer for? My friend told me '3 months' and my other friend told me '6 months!' I said well, I put one in the freezer last night and it was dead this morning .

A woman came to my door and said 'I'm collecting for the local swimming pool, can you help?' So I gave her a bucket of water.

I bought some new slippers the other day, they felt like toast when I put them on!
All burnt and crispy!!!

Guy walks into an Indian restaurant and orders a Chicken Tikka. The waiter brings his meal and says 'enjoy sir'.

But, the meal is sooo spicy he can hardly eat it and calls for the waiter. He says 'I ordered a Chicken Tikka, what is this?'

The waiter says, 'it's not a Chicken Tikka sir, it's a Chicken Tarka... it's Otter.'

Man walks into a pub with a dog under his arm. He says to everyone in the pub 'my dog is a brilliant engineer, if you don't believe me just watch this..' and takes a pair of castration shears out of his pocket. The dog takes one look at them and immediately makes a bolt for the door!

Man goes to church to pray for God to let him win the lottery, he does this every Sunday, not a win at all! After 5 weeks he say to God 'please, please, let me win the lottery, I'm so much in debt and I don't know what to do.'
All of a sudden there is a message comes from God! Do me a favour mate, meet me half way.. buy a ticket!

My great, great, great, Grandad was killed in the battle of the little big horn, well he wasn't actually in the battle! He was camping in the next field and went over to complain about the noise.. and someone shot him!

I was wearing some new aftershave the other day and my girlfriend said 'ohhh that smells nice what is it?' I said, 'Tester.'

I went for a haircut the other day and asked the barber 'how many before me?' He says, '9!' I said 'I'll come back in the morning then.' Same thing happens the next day, I keep saying I'll come back later then. Barber says to apprentice 'go follow him and see where he goes.' Barber says to apprentice 'did you manage to follow him?' He says 'yes!' 'Where does he keep going to then?' he said 'your house!'

English man Scotsman and Irish man all want to go to the Olympic Games but don't have tickets to get in! English man says 'don't worry, watch this' and sees a long washing line pole at the side of the road and picks it up, puts it on his shoulder and says to security 'John Smith, pole vaulter!' Security say 'oh, ok' and let him through.
Scots man finds a big lead ball at the side of the road, holds it in his hand and says 'Hamish McTavish, shot putter.' Security say 'oh, ok, go through'. Paddy finds some barbed wire at the side of the road, puts it under his arm and says Paddy Murphy, Fencing.

Our local butcher got the sack this morning! He was caught putting his willy in the bacon slicer!!! She was also sacked.

American shares a taxi with me along the seafront in Blackpool and we pass South Pier, he says 'how long did it take to build that?' I said 'it took 200 men and about 6 months to build!' He says, 'in America it would take half the men and half the time to build that.' I said 'ok.' Then we passed Central Pier, he said to me, 'how long to build that one?' I said, '300 men and 7 months to build Central Pier', he said, 'in America it would take us half that time and half the men.' I said 'ok'. We got to Blackpool Tower and he said to me 'whats that?' I said 'I don't know, it wasn't there this morning!'

I was driving along the motorway today and my mum phoned me and said 'it's been on the news just now that a mad man is driving down the wrong side of the motorway, be careful'. I said 'one!!!, they're all driving the wrong way'.

I came in from work the other day to find my girlfriend sat on the settee with her feet in a bucket of disinfectant. I said, 'what are you doing?' She said, 'its been on the news just now about the foot and mouth beef scare, is back again!' I said, 'well why are you sat there like that?' She said, Emmerdale Farm is coming on the TV soon and I'm not taking any chances.'

Man takes a photo of his grandad to the photo shop and says 'with the tech' you have nowadays, can you take off his hat? All the photos I have of my grandad he's always got his hat on! I would like one of him without his hat and was hoping you could do it for me.'
Photo man says, 'sure, which way did your grandad part his hair?'
Man says, 'well, you will see that when you take the hat off!'

Guess who I bumped into in the opticians the other day? Everybody.

My friend is on a diet and said to me 'I've lost 5 pounds this week!' I said, 'I lost 5 pounds as well, but it was out of my wallet.'

Another friend says 'I lost a stone this week!' I said 'me too! But I lost the stone out of my engagement ring.'

I bought a jigsaw puzzle today I managed to complete it in two hours, I took it back to the shop with a big smile on my face. The woman behind the counter said 'what are you looking so pleased about?' I said, 'I've completed this jigsaw in 2 hours. She said, 'so what's so good about that?' I said, 'well, it says 'up to 2 and a half years' on the box!'

My Grandma died at her 100th birthday party.. she died half way through them giving her the bumps.

I asked my Irish friend paddy 'where is the Irish channel?' He said 'it's two buttons down from BBC 1.'

How does Bob Marley like his donuts?
Wi jammin.

The Irish Olympic swimming team have been asked to save water so they have shut down lanes 2, 4 and 6 in the swimming pool.

I went to Blackpool on holiday and left my cat with the next door neighbour to look after while I was away. After a couple of days I called him and asked 'how's my cat?' He said 'it's dead, mate.' I said OMG, that's a terrible shock, why didn't you let me down gently? You could have said something like 'well it was playing with a ball on the roof and it slipped but I nursed it for a couple of days but then sadly it died peacefully in it's sleep.' Neighbour says oh OK sorry. Then I asked 'by the way, hows me mum?...
'Well, she was playing with this ball on the roof...'

Question: What's the difference between Hamish McTavish and Walt Disney?

Answer: Hamish McTavish comes from Scotland and Walt Disneey.

Man goes into fish shop and says to lady behind counter 'fish and chips twice please', lady says 'I heard you the first time'.

I called into the doctors to tell him about the tablets he gave me to keep my strength up! I told him I couldn't get the top off the bottle.

Two fellas in prison talking, one says 'how long you in here for?' He answers '4 days'. Fella says 'how did you manage that?' He says 'they hang me on Monday'.

I dreamt I had eaten a giant marshmallow the other day, when I woke up my pillow had gone.

Its the last time I'm ordering frogs legs in the French restaurant I go to! They kept kicking my peas off my plate.

For Sale!
Irish parachute,
opens on impact.

2 Irish men broke into a betting shop and came out having lost £50 each.

Irish man got a pair of skis for his birthday, spent 2 years looking for a lake with a slope.

Paddy and Murphy go deep sea diving, Paddy shouts up to Murphy through the intercom, 'quick get me up, a sharks bitten my leg off!!!' Murphy says 'which one?' Paddy says 'I don't know, there's hundreds of them'.

Paddy goes into a betting shop and says 'can you back horses in here?' Man behind counter says 'of course'. Paddy whistles to his horse and says 'come in, back in now'.

Someone asked me if I was a comedian! I said 'yes I am!' He said 'go on then, change colour!'

Irish man walking down the street with his front door under his arm, he bumps into his wife and she says, 'what are you doing with our front door under your arm?'
He says, 'I'm taking it for a new lock to be put on!'
Wife says, 'how am I going to get in the house now?'
He says, 'I've left a window open for you.'

Whats green?
It's massive?
It's got six legs and
if it falls out of a
tree it will kill you?

A snooker table.

What do you call
a woman with a
pint of beer on
her head?

Beatrix.

What do you
call a woman
with a pint
of beer on
her head
playing pool?
Beatrix
potter.

What do you call a camel without a hump?

Humphrey.

What do you call a fish with no eye?
A Fsh.

What do you call a bear with no ears?
a B

What do you call a deer with no eyes?

No idea.
What do you call a deer with no legs?
...Still no idea

A man gets stopped by the police. Policeman says, 'have you been drinking?' Driver says, 'yes!' Policeman says 'blow into this device!' Driver says 'why? Don't you believe me?'

What do you call a man underneath a car?
Jack

What do you call a bag full of soil ?
Pete.

Man walking along beach says to his friend "I never attract any women on here!"

His friend says, "try putting a potato down your swimming trunks, it works every time."

So he does and walks along the beach!

But, it's even worse, people are laughing at him now!

His mate says to him, "you're supposed to put the potato down the 'front' of your trunks not the 'back'!"

I have a gate that tells the time! Every time I come in from the pub my neighbours shout out to me..
"4 o'clock in the morning!!!"

My girlfriend said to me yesterday, "where have you been?"
I said, "I've been for a game of darts with the lads."
She said "what.. for 3 days?"

Did you know you can't get a job as an airline pilot if your name is Jack? If someone comes into the cockpit and says Hi Jack, everyone starts screaming.

You also can't get a job as a pilot if your name is Ivor Handgranade.

What do you call a Japanese car thief?
Tommy Tuk-a-mota

A referee walks into a bar!
I thought, 'its all going to kick off now.'

Man came up to me and said, "whatever you do, don't mention deodorant to my wife!"
I said, "don't worry I won't, Mums the word."

Velcro!!!! What a rip off.

A friend of mine found a gold coin in a lump of earth! Lucky sod.

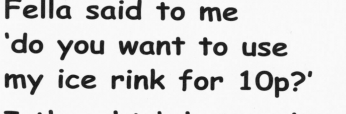

Fella said to me
'do you want to use
my ice rink for 10p?'
I thought 'what a cheapskate.'

Ive got a
horse that
doesn't go
out much!
He's a shire
horse.

I've got a
horse called
Treacle!
He's got
golden
stirrups.

My Grandfather got the
passion for drawing in the war,
he got hit by a doodlebug.

I bought a DVD and at the end of it in the extras it said 'deleted scenes'. When I looked there was nothing there!

I have a friend who has a butler with his left arm missing! Serves him right.

I went into a music shop to buy a violin! Man said, "do you require a bow also." I said, "don't bother wrapping it."

I bought an 85 inch flat screen TV for £50 with the volume stuck on full! At that price I could not turn it down.

I said to my girlfriend "ohhh.. look you're on the TV!!!... Interference!!!

What do you call a pig that does karate?

A pork chop!

Why couldn't the pony sing a lullaby?

Because it was a little horse.

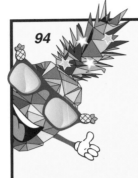

I shouldn't be drinking with what I've got! Man says to me, 'what have you got?' I said, '50 pence'.

I asked my girlfriend, "can you sew a shirt on this button for me please?"

What do Alexander The Great and Winnie The Poo have in common?
They both have the same middle name!

My girlfriend said that I acted like a detective too much and said she wanted to split up! I said "good idea, that way we can cover more ground."

Someone offered me a job this week!!! I said, "don't you threaten me!"

I've changed energy supplier from lucozade to Red Bull, I slept like a baby last night, I woke up screaming for my Mum, and pooed the bed.

A Yorkshire man's dog dies and he decides to have a gold statue made of it. Man making the statue says, "do you want it 18 carrot", he said "no, chewing a bone, ya daft bugger."

I wondered why the ball was getting bigger?

And then it hit me!!

I told my doctor that I'd broken my arm, in 2 places. He said, "well stop going to those places, you fool!!"

I started a band called 999 megabites, we still haven't got a gig yet.